ornithologies

W. H. Erskine Huntington

ANHINGA PRESS

ornithologies

JOSHUA POTEAT

2004 ANHINGA PRIZE FOR POETRY

Selected by Campbell McGrath

ANHINGA PRESS, 2006
TALLAHASSEE, FLORIDA

Cover art: from the collection of Joshua Poteat
Author photo: Allison Titus
Cover design, book design, and production: C. L. Knight
Typesetting: Jill Ihasz
Type Styles: titles and text set in Lapidary 333

Library of Congress Cataloging-in-Publication Data
Ornithologies by Joshua Poteat — First Edition
ISBN — 0938078-90-9 (978-0-938078-90-6)
Library of Congress Cataloging Card Number — 2005935582

This publication is sponsored in part by a grant
from the Florida Department of State,
Division of Cultural Affairs, and the Florida Arts Council.

Anhinga Press Inc. is a nonprofit corporation dedicated wholly
to the publication and appreciation of fine poetry.

For personal orders, catalogs and information write to:
Anhinga Press
P.O. Box 10595
Tallahassee, Florida 32302
Web site: www.anhinga.org
E-mail: info@anhinga.org

Published in the United States
by Anhinga Press
Tallahassee, Florida
First Edition, 2006

for Allison

CONTENTS

ACKNOWLEDGMENTS

Thanks to the editors and readers of the following journals, in which these poems first appeared, sometimes in slightly different versions.

Antietam Review: "The Nostalgia of the Finite"

Bellingham Review: "Documenting the Birds: Office Park"

Blackbird: "Fahrenheit Meditation," "The Stigmata Rather Than a Punch on the Nose," "Burning Instead of Beauty," "Nocturne: for the Doves," "Hitchhiking in the Dying South," "Our Memory, the Shining Leaves"

Crazyhorse: "From the 1941 Catalogue of Dover Books"

Columbia: "Self-portrait as the Autumn of the Red Hat," "Self-portrait as the Autumn I Have Lost"

Diagram: "Meditation for the Dead Swiss"

Greensboro Review: "Nocturne: For the Aviaries"

Gulf Coast: "The Angels Continue Turning the Wheels of the Universe Despite Their Ugly Souls," "Grass Meditation"

Lit: "Letter to Allison with Musical Notation of Hawk"

Lullwater Review: "People Who'd Kill Me (Spain, 1939)"

Marlboro Review: "Sonata for an Open Window"

Nebraska Review: "Nocturne: For the Night Workers of the South," "Nocturne: For the River"

River City: "Meditations in the Margins of the Book of Irish Curses I, III, V, VII, and IX,"

Washington Square: "Meditations in the Margins of the Book of Irish Curses VIII"

42 Opus: "Meditation for Everything We Have Loved"

64: "Just for You"

Several of these won the 2004 National Chapbook Award from the Poetry Society of America, judged by Mary Oliver: "Meditations in the Margins of the Book of Irish Curses," "Fahrenheit Meditation," "Damnatio Memoriae," "From the 1941 Catalogue of Dover Books," and "Grass Meditation."

"Nocturne: for the Aviaries" and "People Who'd Kill Me (Spain, 1939)" also appeared in the book and international traveling exhibition *Pivot Points: Three Generations of Painters and Poets.*

The series "Meditations in the Margins of the Book of Irish Curses I-IX" won the Rella Lossy Award from San Francisco State University/American Poetry Archives.

Grateful acknowledgment to the following for fellowships/monetary awards/time that enabled me to complete this work: Virginia Commonwealth University, Virginia Commission for the Arts, *Blackbird: A Journal of Literature and the Arts*, Vermont Studio Center, Poetry Society of America, *American Literary Review*, *Columbia*, *River City*, *Marlboro Review*, *Bellingham Review*, *Nebraska Review*, *Lullwater Review*, *Yemasse*, Universities West Press, San Francisco State University's Poetry Center/American Poetry Archives, University of Arizona's Poetry Center, Writers' Conferences and Centers, Catskill Writing Workshop, Aquent, and BrannRMG.

And lastly, thank you to everyone who helped me along the way ...

My teachers in one form or another who (in)directly influenced and supported this manuscript: Paula Champa, Adam Chiles, Greg Donovan, Mary Flinn, Philip Gerard, Kathleen Halme, Robert Hobbs, Larry Levis, Andrew Miller, Darren Morris, James Poteat, Gary Sange, Alexis Shein, Marsha Southwick, Gerald Stern, Allison Titus, and Ellen Bryant Voigt.

The judges of contests who somehow noticed: Campbell McGrath, Marvin Bell, Stephen Dobyns, Richard Howard, David Lee, Mary Oliver, Nicole Cooley (twice!), Jon Anderson and the University of Arizona's Poetry Center, Pimone Triplet, Barbara Hamby, *Nebraska Review* editors, and *Yemasse* editors.

Lynne Knight, Rick Campbell, and everyone at Anhinga.

My dear family and friends.

My dearest Allison.

And of course, Ruben.

ornithologies

Be with me, Whitman, maker of catalogues:
For the world invades me again.
— T. Roethke

My pencil gave birth to a family of cripples.
— John James Audubon, *Ornithological Biography,* 1831

FOR THE AVIARIES

NOCTURNE: FOR THE DOVES

On the side of a desert road
            a headless dove,
      its body a basket of ants,
            basket of creosote stems.

To live at all is to grieve
            and from what life
      did we gain this trust,
            awake each dawn

to find the bright air
            full again,
      rustle and coo
            in the widening palms?

NOCTURNE: FOR THE RIVER

I can't bear to be forgotten by any more people,
      and walking home under these anonymous street lamps

it would be easy to slip under the cobblestones
      and sleep away the nights, comfortable and alone.

Even the street lamps have forgotten me,
      forgotten how to give their light,

the sickly powder-orange of a child's mouth
      full of aspirin is all they can muster now. It's sad,

yes, but it's also a little too ... participatory.
      There's no avoiding them, no resemblance

to the living, to the morning light they mimic.
      There's a Buddhist proverb:

Participate joyfully in the sorrows of the world,
      and I've tried, believe me, smiling the pink smile

of a lamb, a quarter in a blind girl's cup,
      but does it mean to breathe in this airy version

of asbestos or to keep walking these streets,
      smashing each light to reclaim some small, hidden

memento from a time when there was hope?
      Tonight, a south wind brings me the scent

of the tobacco plant across the river,
      and the bread factory a few blocks away

has given up its loaves to the air,
      which redeems us in a way, I think,

for redemption is nothing more
          than a breaded wind pulling a night from frailty.

Tell me, Robert E. Lee, of the hundred-year sleep,
          of mice skulls in owl dung, your bronze head

bearing the weight of catacombs hidden
          in the itch of amputees, gas-lit, forlorn.

Tell me, J.E.B. Stuart, that everything will be okay,
          that your horse is facing north because

she misses the snowy fields.
          Tell me, sad horse, with doves nesting

under your raised hoof, in this century of longing,
          how can I go on loving this ruined excuse for a city,

sleepy-sweet night, sweet cicada,
          sweet oak, sweet old nothing?

Sad-eyed Matthew Brady, come down to me
          from your glass-plated heaven of iodine,

from your tent-city of wagons in a muddy field
          where my apartment building now stands,

years of smoke rising between us,
          and watch the reflection of crows

roost far below the water in the tulip trees
          as Whitman did once after the war,

from a skiff in the shallows of the James,
          pale gold, the play of light

coming and going, bats and thrushes
        alive with stars, woven over the musical trees

and over the past, over the milky blossoms
        of wild carrot, or, oblivion.

And so, like the river in the distance
        humming the trestle-song of night trains,

its skin seeming to hold twilight, delay it,
        I stand among these street lamps

a forgotten man, and let the South's last summer
        rise up and consume me.

NOCTURNE: FOR THE AVIARIES

Then the rain came,
      full of a sadness I've never seen before,
through the cottonwoods
      and along the river,
which is no longer a river
          but an apparition under the sand.

Had I five hummingbirds,
      I would make a love charm
and string them from the tongue
      of a small copper bell in those branches,
          necks hovered together, broken.

Had I a swan, it would sleep
      under the hives
with a bucket of fresh milk,
          with the splintered white faces of goats.

To reclaim or take apart the night,
      like the city does, carving through
the blind river?
          The brilliant debris of stars, the air?

Nothing in this world is ours.

NOCTURNE: FOR THE NIGHT WORKERS OF THE SOUTH

Once, when I was young and loved every girl that breathed
        the same summer air as I did, I worked as a night watchman
in the county asylum, a forgotten place, lost among

the kudzu, the long-leaf pines birthing cones the size
        of watermelons. It was the kind of place that, when it rained,
spotted-moth larva would tunnel from the wet plaster ceilings

and drink the patient's ears. The county wanted it forgotten,
        their own kind gone bad, like in the Bible, where Christ
slaps rotting eggs from the yellow mouths of lepers.

Eat of this bread, he said, or something close, and the lepers
        scraped up the eggs and made a sandwich, and I imagine for
the first time, Christ shrugged. *You are what you eat*,

he should have said, if he had any truth left in him by then.
        I wasn't allowed to talk to the patients, and usually,
they were all medicated by the time I hitched a ride

there, on the backs of flatbeds wedged between crates
        of sweet potatoes rotting under the moon.
When I found out that I wasn't really a night watchman

but an owl catcher, and would have to incinerate any owl
        I caught, I stayed on anyway. I needed the work.
According to legend, seeing a Horned Owl during a meal

was supposed to mean, *Don't finish your stew.*
        Barn Owls seen more than a mile or so from their perches
were wandering ghosts, or meant that ghosts

would soon force themselves into your dreams,
        a madness I could do without.
Sighting a Snowy Owl meant bones would ache

but without further consequence. They would simply ache
        for a while, then stop. I found this applied for all owls.
My whole body ached then. When I dressed for work

it was like dressing a wound. I couldn't tell if it was the girls
        or the birds. I became good at it, though, despite the ache,
if that is even possible, chewing the stolen, orange meat

of potatoes to keep me awake, slumped in the attics
        with a canvas bag from the laundry room.
Christ also said, *Any true work is done alone*. This I believe.

The sweat of the insane is sweeter than ours:
        clover and bee's wing and honeyed ham.
I could hear them breathing beneath me in their beds. Don't ask how

it was to be so near that bleak sea of faces. It's the faces, paint flaking off,
        dolls with blinking eyes, snow of paint in spilled urine.
Even their white breath, eight-petaled in the chill of their rooms,

was something I couldn't name.
        Dogwood: no. Wild pea: perhaps ... but no. Chamomile,
milk-weed: never. I never looked at them, the pink azalea of hair

between their legs, luminous with lice, not even down
        the blouses of the nurses when they bent to look in
at the big-headed owls. Now, I think I brought those birds

down through the wards, alive and flapping,
        so someone would stop me. No one ever gets tired of the moon.
No one ever said, *Fuck the moon, let's get it out of here*.

We keep it around, we learn to like it.
        Habit is the devil's glorious invention, like I heard war could be.
Easing a bayonet into a belly was the same as opening

a can of tomatoes by firelight if you did it enough.
        These were birds and I burned them and on rare days
I remember their heads, round and milky, baby's breath,

their wings not really wings, finally, but damp bolts of silk,
        and the low sough of wind dragging their ashes into September's arms.
I remember the story of General Lee on his deathbed

telling a sad friend to cheer up, that he had known
        but three happy hours during his whole existence.
Two of those as a child asleep in the boughs of a white oak,

the last in an asylum staring at a beautiful girl's naked ribcage
        that had been woven into a basket by tuberculosis.
Night transcends what the proudest day can do, that's for damn sure,

all silently,
        the indescribable night and stars,
far off and silently.

DAMNATIO MEMORIAE

The light that is with us, here, now,
          will ruin us one day —

angelic among the whitened orchards of cloud,

palest blue, the tips of bee's wings
          home from a clover patch.

Perhaps the only time we become angelic
          is over our world — the farthest away
from everything we have ever known —

an ether, a grace, a world that belongs
          not quite to us — but is suddenly inherited,

as twilight inherits the trees, the dead branches

of winter — as the cities far below gather their rivers.

From up here, the clouds seem tethered
          to their shadows, each with a blanket
of its own, tablecloths of walking rain.

Ephemeral, of course — but why put a name on it?

They part the way they deserve to,
          the evening slipping away
beneath them, night's undertow

eroding the blue soil of sky —

kind of like an ocean,
          only deeper.

Call the clouds *white-throated vireos in the new hives,*
      and it wouldn't be enough.

Dead satellites orbiting the five rows of moon,
      is close,

brailled letters of patience swimming the pale reefs,
      is closer.

Each time a plane takes off it is the end, really:
      witness to the end of the world.

Funny, how it happens over and over.

The same flight attendant filing the same red
      fingernails is a disease only the damned can know,

her reddened eyes still asleep in a Denver hotel,
      the same red exit doors, red wing-lights,
wilted cherry blossoms and Coca-Cola

and the red mouths of children sitting too close
      to televisions somewhere below us.

The old woman seated in front of me is asleep.

She could be anyone and because of this
      she is nothing and I like her for it.

Anonymity gives her a certain beauty,
      as does sleep, as does the last bit of sun
glinting from the wing.

Watching her decide whether to leave
          the tiny plastic window shade up or down
was enough to convince me that one day long ago

a man gathered a crown of lilacs from a ditch
          to put in her hair

and she looked at them so closely and full of wonder,
          the man knew he had it made, already
owned the pearl buttons on her blouse

but she was counting the aphids gorging
          on the stems, smiling a little

at their ruined, indifferent hearts.

Between the crack in these seats, I can see through
          her thinning platinum hair to her pale scalp —

it reminds me of the albino boy
          in my sixth grade class who shaved his own head
so no one would suspect his curse of pigment,

his immense longing for light,

though his scalp glowed the white
          of a chickadee's song and brought upon him
a cruelty I could never bear.

⬛

I heard that naming a cloud is like living one more day
          with an X-ray of your hand filled with buckshot
slipped under the mattress,

hoping that, when the rooms of sleep
　　　　finally eat away the black stars of shrapnel,

your hand will emerge from the bandages white,
　　　　whole, and beautiful again.

I do both in case it's true.

Lenin did it to Trotsky, not with an X-ray,
　　　　but with a photograph. Trotsky is there beside him,
stoic, wrapped in a thick gray coat and hat, and Lenin,

bare-headed on the wooden stage, pointing towards
　　　　a future far off in the hills, and I imagine, the scent
of burned sausage rolling through the square.

Seven years later in the same photo, no Trotsky.
　　　　No hat, either.

Just an empty space that a cloud couldn't fill,
　　　　a boy in the bottom left corner vomiting into a flour sack,
the lonely arm of Lenin aiming north to a Ukraine

eaten away with peasant graves.

The Romans did it long before Lenin, and were
　　　　more obvious, dramatic, preferring to loan out,

for a small fee, hundreds of bone-chisels
　　　　and let the crowds hack up
the deposed emperors along with their statues.

The emperor's children were spared the chisels
　　　　and instead, given to the lions:

a small, nameless meal:
        a new hunger for the hungry.

Their soft and precious ears strung up on ivy
        took days to dry, and the villagers renamed
the ears to distract the little deaf ghosts:

apricot-halves: sponges: doe-prints-in-sand:
        olive leaves: look! — skipping stones.

The Romans didn't mess around.

They didn't need mattresses,
        or for that matter, clouds.

It seems childish, I guess, to believe
        that to make the body whole

or change the collective memory of history
all you have to do is slip a bit of film
        between mattress and box-spring,
grind a skull into a grayish paste.

From this height, though, I can believe anything,
        even the translation from Latin:

Damnatio Memoriae —

a mere whisper of it is enough to dim the heart,
        turn leaves into smoke. It is simply —

the condemnation of memory.

No more, no less, no introduction, no awl
        or chisel, no star hung from the night's rotting beams,
no hat, no scalp, no cloud, no grave.

Call it whatever you want. It will erase what you love,
        follow you through the frozen streets of oblivion.

It will outlive you.

—

The woman's head in front of me
        lolls sharply to one side.

I would like to hold it up for her, a gentle kite,
        no stories or songs, just my hand for a pillow,
hairspray sticking to my palm.

Easy does it: rest now: head in hand: sleepy doe.

Let's be sentimental for once,
        let's return to the authentic.

The crop circles through the window:
        dinner plates or bruises or transgression
of earth — what does it matter now?

Far off, dusk spreads across the fields,
        yellow-tipped — this absence
is what we have between us,

the heart a clock.

If I held her head in my hands,
        would it save me?

Save me from the memory of the albino boy,
　　　　gullible and pink, as Danny Joye,
the principal's son, pummels him over and over

for no other reason than to erase him,
　　　　a fission of soil and blood,
me looking away and knowing

that I was heartless for not stopping it
　　　　and human for laughing with the rest of them,
at that pale boy who laughed back at us
　　　　in the way a bat blindly echoes through
telephone wire: skin wing: crimson mouth:

under the light of a spring sun bright enough
　　　　to carry all the bees dying in the clover.

———

America is a cloud, by the way — of light
　　　　and shadow and silvered calm.
The nervous chatter of businessmen
　　　　when the plane hits an air pocket
is the kind of sound honored

in the outermost level of hell.

Turbulence, one of the businessmen says,
　　　　reminds me of screwing my secretary
while talking to my wife on the phone

and his associates laugh their ringing coin
　　　　laughs, each remembering a childhood
that seemed more like a documentary film
　　　　on adolescent growth than an intimate life:

testosterone line graphs: vague discolored
        diagrams of genitalia: National Geographic
stuffed under the mattress.

I am no angel here, either — or anywhere —
        too clumsy and dulled to be
that weightless, that azure-eyed.

A little boy sitting beside the old woman
        vomits peanuts into the pilot's hat
which looks nothing like Trotsky's.

The beauty: gone.
        The glinting wings: forgotten.
The sky can make a list of forgetfulness,
        and I've seen this for a fact.
Lover, dearest, pilgrim, carrion,

I will outlive no one. I will erase what I have loved.

The one white sail fluttering below
is a ghost on a trip to the city of ghosts —

rising into the emptiness cities fill —
        pointing its lonely arm towards a night
that will blanket all our graves with its song.

HITCHHIKING IN THE DYING SOUTH

I have seen the morning spread over the fields
       and I have walked on, trying to forget
how it seemed that daybreak was founded
       on the most fragile web of breath,
and I had blown it.

       Then I thought it might not exist at all,
nor had it ever. That it was only the idea of breath
       and the egrets asleep in sourgrass were the idea
of flight, and if I was to breathe in,
       it would all just disappear.

I have seen the spotted toads at dusk
       come up from the ditches after a rainstorm
and into the asphalt's steam and I have seen them
       crushed by lumber trucks, then lifted away
into the pines by the gathering crows.

       I have felt the night quiver with heron's wing
over the swamps, over wild pigs in a blackberry patch,
       their snouts bloody and alive in the moonlight,
and I have walked on, dirty, alone, kicking to the grasses
       the swollen bodies of possum, squirrel, rabbit, raccoon,
giving them no prayer, no peace-filled silence.

       But that was long ago, when work was scarce
and I thumbed my way to the tobacco plant
       or the slaughterhouse, north up Highway 17
to Holly Ridge or down to Bulltail on 210,
       either way I would be shoveling something until dusk,
something soft and warm and beyond me.
       And I would be glad for it.

Walking with that forgotten gesture wavering
       in the morning air, I felt that people

could come into the world to a place
>they could not at first even name,
and move through it finally, like the dawn,
>naming each thing until filled with a buoyancy,
a mist from the river's empty rooms.

>*Thumb of autumn, thumb of locust, thumb of every kissed lip.*

I have seen a cow die under the wheels
>of a Cadillac going sixty, and who's to say
what the cow got from this?
>Some would say a dignity, perhaps,
past the slaughterhouse
>and the carcasses swimming the eaves.

>Or was it a punishment for nudging open
the gate-latch, the driver of the car
>in shock, mouthing *cow, cow,*
and the crows in the pines answering
>with the kind of sympathy my foreman used
when one of his line-workers
>cut off another finger in the shredder.
Son, at least you still got your arm.

>It's difficult to get this straight,
but there was a beauty to the sparks
>that spread out under the car, under the cow,
as they went from flesh to asphalt to flesh again:
>*fireflies in the hollow of the hills:*
a blanket of white petals from the tree of moon.

>A brief and miniature dawn began,
there on a summer night in the South
>I had come to love as part of myself,
the sparks clinging in the grass for a moment,

unbearably bright, a confused moth nuzzling up
to the reflection of a flame shining in
       the cow's one open eye.

Now that I think of it, there was maybe even
       a beauty in the cow's fat, white body, a peace
I would never know, as it took in the car,
       lay down with it: *calf-soft: morning breath.*

This peace had a body, it was caught up in the night,
       made from night, there on the shoulder of a road
so endless even the stars shrugged it off
       and took the sparks as one of their own.

MEDITATIONS IN THE HIGH BRANCHES

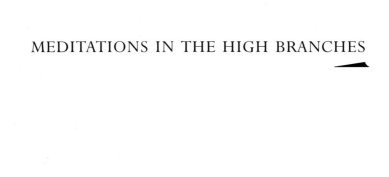

MEDITATION FOR EVERYTHING WE HAVE LOVED

What do you love the most?
        Say the reddish work of death
as it strolls through the fields:
                the peaks of the sky

between the reeds and the stream.
        All our memorable mistakes
easing into us as a bandaged ewe,
                after giving birth, eases

the bloated body of her lamb
        into the marsh with her tongue-prints
on its face. Let it rest.
                Let it become what it will.

Love leaves us dull with nothing else to say
        and whatever is the most will never be enough.
Say *nothing*. Nothing.
                Keep saying it.

It is right there in front of you.
        It will sleep through the damp nights
and suckle its own tiny breast.
                Say *everything*.

MEDITATIONS IN THE MARGINS
OF THE BOOK OF IRISH CURSES

i. In the middle of the field, may your horse kill you

Let it be a roan, without foal, without a crown
       of honeybees circling her mane of clover.
The tongue of a bee is golden and can never
         mourn the evening as it weaves through

the river birches, *Nyssa Aquatica*, named for
       the water that sweetens its touch, and *Pinus Palustrus*,
long-leaf pine, named for the palace of cinder
        above the river. Let it be the roan, please, without

holiness, or shame. May she throw my ribs to the graveyard clay
       and make a cake from my legs of broken air.
May her tail, coarse as an orphan's wrist, sweep the bees
        into my mouth that will never taste the river again.

How can the silence remain whole beneath the grass?
      May she never know how much I loved her.

ii. Your soul to the devil

What farness summons you? What grief?
In my sleep I see you burning.
                  — Laurie Sheck

Nothing that this distant night brings is enough
       to hold back the dawn. The same with the soul,
that orthopedic star, that clubfoot who rents
        the room above us. Our souls are not our own.

We do not own them, and I am comfortable
      with this fact, this one true finality

that can never touch the sweet reply of coal trains
                in the night. For what reason they haunt this air

is not mine to answer. The soul asks for nothing
           and to give it the warmth of a body is to make
it laugh in the dunes of a mind oblivious and beautiful.
                 White heart, white road. See, my friends, there among

the black branches? The sad, voiceless envy
          of the unchanging dead? Doesn't take long at all.

iii. Back from the river, back to the river,
   may savage dogs eat you, one foot on a mountain

This is the landscape I once believed in,
         and because of belief, I have made it across
the frozen river, the marshes torn apart
           by winter, to the disappearing rooms

of the sea. Make me want it: this loveliest
        of air. Make the world another world,
beneath the persimmon grove and the rain.
          I am not hated and I am not lucky, but I know

that when I leave a place the rivers will not
         miss me, and if the owl and bat hunting
among the persimmon briefly touch (talon:
         skin wing) and leave me to myself,

then pray the dogs feast on my gallant feet,
         for the mountain is burning, and I regret none of it.

iv. I Have Tried to Imagine the Kind of City
You and I Could Live in as King and Queen
(Or: May the cats eat the women)

Beyond the cities, bees have inherited
        the ruined walls of barns, so hail to whatever
you found in the sunlight that surrounds us.
                Hail to the bees in their blue walls humming

the song of dead men, which is no song.
        Hail to the pumpkinseed rotting in the embers,
to the red nail on the tongue that said, *May the cats*
            eat the women, to the broken little fish under the docks,

under the ice and light and the failure of it all.
        And if there were grief within this, within all beauty,
then every city would be enough to hold us,
            gathered in the long hours before dawn,

the harbor abandoned, the ships undone by the tide.

v. May you not see the cuckoo nor the corncrake

It could be worse. On Attila the Hun's
        wedding night, he got so drunk he hemorrhaged
from the nose and suffocated to death
           in his own blood. I'm not saying I want

any of this. I've always considered
        myself a victim, though. Haven't you ever
embarrassed yourself? It's embarrassing
           to live sometimes. I've touched a nest of wasps

in the night just to get an idea of how the human
        flame is shaped, and a sparrow joined me, yet I can't
say birds aren't grateful for such a chance, there
                in the darkness that only the leaves own.

I'm living is what this means. Maybe you've noticed.
        The tiny hearts have gathered in the trees.

vi. *The curse of the widows and orphans on you*

There is a kind of peacefulness that exists only after
        the winds stop and the trees on this street come alive
in their silence. I felt that now, the want of my hands
        to become breath against these leaves,

the same leathery magnolias the rum-shod drunks
        on Grace Street weave cups from, stems
looped with sap, tossing petals
                to the pretty girls on their lunch breaks,

a little money jangling in their pockets
        after a day's work at the dry dock.
I want a heaven for us, from a time
        when there was some hope, an abacus

of sparrows asleep in the high branches.
        Only then would I be happy.

vii. May God weaken you

There is a light that fails in my mouth.
                              — *Georg Trakl*

I have seen my face in an autopsy photo, adrift
              in the shroud of 1910. *This light is so much like you,*
I tell myself, under the alcohol lamps and bone curettes.
              Now a cadaver, I can see what it means to be

honey in a tobacco pouch, the skin of God in a firefly's gut.
              The stars' grand indifference is not enough anymore,
that falsest of freedoms. I want to fall on the ice of a frozen river
              and see the grasses swaying in the current beneath.

I want to uncork the ether jars and wash the moths from
              the apothecary's wooden bedpan. Remember when we were
the only ones alive, dear surgeons? The century, neglected, witnessed
              our passing, our cursed days. There we were, weakened

and lost among the tourniquets, the amputated legs of night graceful
              in the wind and in the flesh and in the porous dawn.

viii. The death of the kittens to you

A brace of partridges in a meat-shop window:
              I ask for sorrow on the house of trees.
A red bone in the throat, a red nail on the tongue:
              I ask for twilight in the house of bees.

A pig's snout on her and the dead mouth of a sheep:
              I ask the stars to drown, to yawn, to veil.
A gentle mule abandoned on the road to sleep:
              I ask for dawn, and on the sea, a sail.

So much for the swans under the willows and rain:
        So much for the kittens under the bridge at dusk:
So much for the sky and the sane and the insane:
            So much for spring, my love, let it run. Let it rust.

(A field of garlic, Shepherd's Purse, wild ginger:
        if I could remember, I would, and miss her.)

ix. May the entrails and mansion of
  pleasure out of this worm fall

I feel that we have failed somehow.
        Not the present, not the past, but the absent
way a boy sharpens a stick on the sidewalk
            to stab a sleeping dove. Sure, the light gathers

in the white field of husks and we grow
        accustomed to the dark, but time diminishes
us, settles into the city's incessant furrowing,
            and look where I ended up, drunk in an orchard

of tar and lead, the tobacco factories dead in the air
        and the radio towers across the river broadcasting
the red lights of famine, of sleep. Dear city, I am incapable
        of love. I abandon you to the willows.

Dear city, your breath is glass in my ear, your throat
        a boy, crawling through the long night grasses.

FAHRENHEIT MEDITATION

Must it be this way, the air no longer wet, seamless,
         no longer ours, becoming the cicada's path
from night-blooming cereus to creosote,
            the summer of moth larva rolling in the rice jar?

If so, let the heat rise over these desert mountains,
         rot-filled, and cover this city.
If so, begin with sadness, sadness,
          because it is a good place to start,

because heat is a sadness of its own,
         though I cannot begin to define it,
except for that first awareness as a child,
          that dim ache of the wrist, on a night like this,

years ago in a different south, the silent acknowledgment
         of a thing so spread out and weightless it becomes a landscape
of radio towers across the fields, red lights flickering
          beyond the marsh's conspiratorial hum.

Ask me and I will tell you of the flowering tobacco leaves
         of my youth on fire in the night, lit by lightning,
the sweet wind pushing the flames
          toward the tree-break and into the stables

where my father sat on a three-legged stool birthing a foal.
         To see night burning is to see God, or a minor version:
angelic palette, grub-white cataracts of summer.
          To see Father is to see night long for the sea.

This is how we live within,
         concubined to the land.
White peacocks aflame can sing the song
          of flight, I think, of rain and June:

ash-plumed amniotic sac:

> *manure shoveled into the cantaloupe rows.*

Alexander the Great, after observing the depths
> of the ocean from a glass barrel said, *Sir Barons,*
I have just seen that this whole world is lost,
> *and the great fish mercilessly devour the lesser.*

Call me lesser then, I don't mind it.
> Call me lost.

This morning an airplane lifted over the city, the ghost
> of a pale child's toy, and left this desert behind.
A cactus wren danced mid-flight with a cicada,
> danced, yes, but truth, too, and even a certain perfectness,

both catching the last breath of early light,
> both filled with a promise,
to not give in, to die in this air a truthful death,
> in this land that should never be ours.

The hunger of fire becomes a landscape of its own,
> *an alternate world: to harvest, to harvest.*

My father mutinied the mother mare
> and took the foal to the marsh, delicate like a kite,
and drowned her.
> So what if the moon sang of its rising then?

I was courageous, wind-strong,
> I grew to fit that brackish air,
three-syllable morning
> through the pines.

Later, he walked the fields with me in his arms,
   over the roasted copperheads, spun me
through that black sea, a smoke sail tied on
    with handkerchief dabs. This would be our life.

Black: it hurt to look at it. Empty: I had to love it,
   and he held my wrist against a stalk blue as plum,
still smoldering, so I couldn't forget,
    so that heat stayed with me forever.

GRASS MEDITATION

i. Deer in the Grass

Ghost, come closer.
                    — T. Roethke

It is better to have nothing,
for at last even our bones will fall.
I tell you this, deer,
because you die so well,
and yet, transcendence aside,
press the tips of the moving grass
with an indifference made for men,
for the wind tonguing the frost.
Here we are, deer. Get up.
Tell us how to live.
Even the rim of gnats reeling
your honeycombed brain want to know.
I once thought that nothing
could ever die. Walking through
these suburbs at twilight,
front lawns glowing,
each sprinklers' Morse code
a pattern that could save us all,
a sweet clatter of bats in the cherry trees ...
who could leave a place like this?
Deer, come closer. Ignore the ruin.
You won't be loved through
the long rains. Remember the foxes
wading the river, so alive in their dusk,
in their murderous little worlds.
I watched you live a life among the grasses:
your small bone feet,
your toes all fallen like petals.

ii. Common Names of Dune Grass (Festuca Mollis)

Pintongue, repose, sandhair, sweet
thumbs, angel bed, pillow grass, lissome.
To go from disorder to order
in moments with the glorious naming:
that voice, pure in the mind's wide,
gasping easement ... that paraffin
of Latinless joy, twilight bats
feeding on fireflies.
What gave us the mouth to hold
the water of these nights?
What gave us the wound?
Some would say the soul,
but the docks in the distance,
and even the mud under them,
are filled with a light
I cannot seem to find in the living.
And the sea, indolent, fish-eyed,
washes the hooves of wild horses,
scarred from barnacle and clam.
It is this that wounds, that brings us
to our knees: the solitude of a foal
sleeping under the shore pines,
the warmth of its breath ... starry campion ...
wild pea ... is all we could ever want.
So *Festuca Mollis*, keep it to yourself.
I'll name the ghosts alone tonight,
because the earth, goddamnit,
the earth provides.

iii. The Suffering of Grass

is not suffering at all.
It is of itself, and does nothing

but sway, the wind a way to touch,
finally, after a hundred mornings of silence.
In his journals, Petrarch asked himself,
Don't you think grass deserves better?
It was Petrarch who also said, *Life never finishes,*
after meeting Siamese twins in a monastery,
their bone hearts torqued together,
their hands fluttering like doves.
Early in his own life he refused to love
any child, wincing at every little foot
in his front yard. It was the grass he loved,
and determined, through the sweet rot
of cuttings, that it does feel,
and thus suffers, mostly.
Anything that rots, suffers.
If we must go, let it be by flame.
If we must go, let this earth grow
to grass again. Or not.
Lying here in my neighbor's
perfect viridian expanse,
I admit to feeling nothing,
even though just last week,
a mockingbird in the shriveled
longleaf pine sang the first eight notes
to *You and the Night and the Music,*
and I sighed at the sound,
thinking of Petrarch asleep
on the lawns of his youth,
so fed up and devious, never knowing
that the way to the earth's vastness is not
through the front yards
or the suffering of grass,
but to be sure we remain whole and pale
in the sky of our one true life.

MEDITATION FOR THE DEAD SWISS

There is nothing more normal than the Swiss. There is no reason for them
to die, so they are more terrifying in a way. They are us.
— *Christian Boltanski*

This much we understand: the desire of
                    not wanting to die, of avoiding death
as much as possible. Which is the same.

Which is: how it rises, how it widens.

How, if the winds drag another shutter open
                    then it is only air that holds us above the billow
of clotheslines: chimney-slant, open-winged.

And if this is the end, hand us a blanket
                    and sing about the city, its smoke of brick
and knife fights on the wharves.

This we understand: each thing is of itself.
        Each thing is its end.

In the cupped palm of a cup: at the corner
of corners: in the light of light, we stand
                    on roofs in the rain and watch the clouds move
through the city because it is this
that lets us move on.

The delicate map of breath on a window
is no longer ours when it leaves us.

                    The skin of a plum, the inside of a mouth.

We hang on so tight to them our fingers
mold into their shapes and we become them:

a violin's case open and empty,
a cloth to wipe the sweat, the rosin.
Penciled marks to remember
                     where to pause, where to end ...

You and I, we want the same thing, the same ending.
And in this wanting lies a failure
                     to see clearly, straight to the thing,
to the light that illuminates us
on the street, crouching low
against the walls of a pub in a strange country.

          Maybe Switzerland, maybe not.

Either way, we are drunk in the rain.
The knives in our pockets begin to sing
                     and we know the cobblestones are not ours,
the doors to the barrel-maker's warehouse
are open but they are not ours

and the want bursts in our pockets
                     like a plum as we sit and mumble
about the weather, about our lives.

And we hate each other for not dying.
          And for dying.

TROPPO VERO
OR, GLASS EYE IN A RAVEN'S MOUTH

SELF-PORTRAIT AS THE AUTUMN OF THE RED HAT

To begin with the hat would be foolish.
  The story goes back further, to the fox
standing over a dead hare in an open field,
  to hunting muskrat in the Cohansey marshes
and finding the body of a white-haired girl
  in a heron's nest, her mouth wide and full
of mud. The hat has nothing to do with it,
  at least from what I can tell. We're poling
through the bulrush and we run aground,
  but it's not aground, it's her. There was a hat, yes,
and it was hers, but it was found much later
  washed under the old docks, limp, a sadness
beyond any of us, cold in the heart's distance
  of our failed autumn.

PEOPLE WHO'D KILL ME (SPAIN, 1939)

The beekeeper's daughter. With a sack full of bees.
She'll come in, quiet, from the orchards, figs in her shawl
and gather the bees from their white boxes.

And Professor Garcia, the music instructor. With bare hands.
In his empty house, he'll play his piano and each note
will be one of my fingers in a jar.

Maybe even Juan, with his pocket knife, but he was taken
by the police for carving *Viva l'* ... into a fence and not telling them
how he would finish the sentence. He said there was no sentence
to begin with, then saluted them: *Mierde! May you fall
into a nettle-patch. May your children become dust.*

He's the kind of guy who could kill you, and then drink a cup of rum,
or take a bath. It wouldn't bother him.

One morning he heard voices in the town well,
so he lowered four baby pigs and cut the rope.
Perfect. He was perfect in a way only he could be.
The type of perfect that makes you ache, that keeps you
awake at night, listening for the steam engine's gentle hiss
or the assassin's snores on the roof.

*A loaf of stale bread for the pigs in the well. A pocket knife
in each of their bellies.* He would definitely kill me.
But she, oh she would kill me. And mean it.

Her father's white boxes of bees ... I watched her bathe in the lake
beyond the hills: the evening light folded around her.
Yes. The evening light.

The fires in the potato fields folded into her,
and I tried to think of what love meant to me then,
if her nakedness was a chore I could finish and forget,
like combing the goats, stitching the horse's rump.

It hurts to say this. I took her blouse, the simple white one.

The hills opened up and I'd like to think the villages were quiet for miles.
Four buttons, one missing. I needed to smell what she couldn't give me:
the dark cup of her breasts, the slight nuzzle of her shoulder.
I wore that shirt under my own. I wasn't confused, just dying.
And she'll kill me for that, coming through the orchards,
barefoot, me asleep against a fence beside the road.

A sack of bees over my head. Simple and perfect.
A shirt of bees, breathing them in. The pain would be immense.
Professor Garcia weeping over his piano. Juan handing the assassin a pear.
I would want to die this way.

THE ANGELS CONTINUE TURNING THE WHEELS
OF THE UNIVERSE DESPITE THEIR UGLY SOULS
(MALVERN HILL BATTLEGROUND)
          — *after Alice Aycock*

There is truth in the phrase, *the dead are at ease under the fields.*

Autumn is what seizes it. A field of dried cotton stalks
          have a grace in the wind only the dead can love,
and so, belief comes simple, rendering not a season
          but stalk against stalk,

poor cousin-song of crickets,
          poor furrow-in-the-gut, little nothing-at-all.

At least it will snow soon, goes the cotton's rattled melody,
          and this field beyond the city, flooded by night,
turns blue in the first frost as the ghosts of past crops
          bridle upon it.

I give the field ghosts, and the wind eggs them on —
          corn and sweet potato, tobacco and bean —
hovering the mule-plough of two hundred years.

So much for truth.

It's the least I can do since I cannot for the life of me
          think of anything but the thin curtains of a hospital room
and an X-ray of my crooked spine pinned to a wall of light,

the sweet milk of vertebrae, my own skull
          frowning back at me, such a cold cup of jaw,
so white I could have easily drunk myself.

What a desire, to take one's self in, to unravel
        the body's red yarn shapes and deceive the plague
of boundless hunger, to imagine this cotton field as bone
        ready for the gin, rib and wrist and collar,

all tenderhearted stars,
        inexact, held up to the light of no moon, no cloud.

This is me scattered in the furrows, I thought.
This is me, marrowless and fluff, grub-eaten.

I don't believe in much. Not the descent and re-ascent
        of the soul ... the palace of the kingdom of the dead ...

So much for desire.

I have seen those X-rays of Velasquez, the hidden layers
        illuminated to reveal six ghost-versions of hands along the rim
of an egg bowl, six different plates of fish and garlic,
        a dwarf's blind face formed into the severed head of a pig,
then back to a dwarf, leaving the pig's wondrous eyes.

A bird later becomes a peach in the mouth of a jug,
        and this is how I feel about the world at the moment.

Troppo vero, said Pope Innocent in a letter
        to Velasquez of his portraits. *Too faithful.*

Representation is all we are in the end, I guess, and then some.

Charred ivory: muller stone: horse-hair:
        white lead: madder: massicot.
This is me.

It is almost winter, here in the leftover cotton
        that once held the thousand luminous angels of desire
as they curled inward towards a truth

unlike any flame they had seen.

This must be how the soldiers slept,
        with the night all around them
and their bodies knowing where it was.

And this must be how the deer moved
        over the fields long after the battle, drinking frost
from the eyes of the dead with their small pink tongues.

Oh dwarf, oh king, oh skeleton of mine,
        will I ever feel your wings between my hands again?

OUR MEMORY, THE SHINING LEAVES
(WATERFORD FAIR CIVIL WAR REENACTMENT)

From here it's hard to tell who's killing who
and I guess it's better this way,
not knowing the difference between the gray and the blue
and the stillness that answers each rifle shot with the only phrase
stillness can ever imagine itself saying:
at last we are here together.

It's an indulgent thought and that's why stillness never works.
It's too comfortable, too secure. I think you would agree
but I feel dumb asking because what good are questions
as the evening falls across our faces and the black oaks
at the edge of the field take on a pale yellow light
that the end of summer brings and the soldiers dying
their solemn deaths in front of us begin to believe
too much in themselves, in the blank crisp volley
of their voices: a decayed stone wall separating then and now.
It is to this that we should listen:
the space between the air and our bodies.

We don't belong here among the dead.
That is what they are, right? Trying to remember
is a kind of dying. Each pull of the trigger an elegy
for the body of a boy found by Union troops
in the ruined chimney of Gaines Mill,
for a photograph in a child's history book
of a field surgeon lunging with his amputating saw
at two dogs fighting over a canvas bag of opium.
How much simpler does it get?

Stillness says *at last we are here* but we shouldn't be.
You are too beautiful and I am too careless to want any of this.
The funnel cake, the candy apples, stove-pipe hats and horse-drawn carts
full of pumpkins and the brown cloth of dusk. The land rising slowly
into the pines, into the mountains, leaving the brittle grass lining the creek

and the town and the town's shadow behind in their silence: a silence
we're all used to, that we can't shake off and if we do, it's not us
that does the shaking. It's a cricket hopping from the grass to your knee,
the last day of summer and all we can do is wait for something to happen.
And it does. But never the way we want it.

Never the sudden sparrow there on your foot snipping the cricket
in two before it opens its big mouth. No, the cricket chirps and right there
summer unfolds and evening begins and you cup the poor dark song
in your hand and let it go.
It's not real, a father says to his boy sitting on a bale of hay

behind us. *They're not dying.*
I look at him and know that for once in his life he is right.
The sad flinch that fathers give the world when their children
are shown too much or not enough makes him seem almost distant,
not wholly there, a part of the landscape and I begin to regret looking at him
as we regret anything that is crumbling right before us:
the ocean's shore: the shriek of the fox diffused by leaves.

It's too soon to know that flinch, though I have felt myself
holding it back at certain times. Not now, though, not here ...
then you grab my hand, working each finger
into mine as if to say, *It's real, believe me.*
Then maybe we should be here, if that's how it has to be, to prove
that we belong with the evening and the oaks and the dead gathering in piles
under the hay, with the boy who now has learned that death
is as comic and terrible as a sheep in a petting zoo,
the oily grit from its coat still there on his fingers,
a texture that stillness can never imagine.

The difference is that these soldiers eventually get up.
They brush the thistle and the straw from each other's backs,
not sure exactly of where they are for a moment,

and they walk away jingling their car keys and stretching their legs,
stiff from being dead so long: *at last and together*.
The difference is that the boy searches the field after the skirmish
looking for a trace of what he saw (gold button: hank of hair:
glass eye in a raven's mouth) and finds nothing but a hungry sparrow
lifting him into our memory, into the shining leaves.

We should be used to this sort of thing by now.
We should walk towards the white barn on the hill
where the lambs bite and snort at the children who get too close,
and forget about everything. Fold up the day into our sweaters,
hold each other closer than night or stillness can get.
And as the light carries us to the hill as though
we are flying into ourselves, shouldn't we finally,
after all of this, understand our lives?
Shouldn't we say what we meant to say?

FROM THE 1941 CATALOGUE OF DOVER BOOKS

i. Uniforms of the American Revolution Coloring Book

I apologize on behalf of the dead.
        They do not mean to hurt us.

      They show us a way to be in the world,
          then leave us for the deer and salt licks,
the reed-shrouded fog in the marsh.

I knew a dead person once,
        and I consider myself lucky.

To wear the ghost of him
    like an untanned bear hide brought me
        a secret pleasure I have not felt since.

Who needs lungs when you're flying
        among the trees?

    It's what the taxidermists all say:
      We construct the infinite spirit
and you ignore the palpable soul.

Think of it.

To wear the uniform of the dead
      is to walk through mountains.

    Show me the way to the doorless sea,
      to the river of brine and day,

and I'll give you hands to breathe again, lads,

    the most important things you'll need
    to cradle this land
      that will never be yours.

ii. How to Know the Wild Fruits

There comes a point when the wild fruits
        are unknowable, their small heads turning
away from us when the wind is right and warm,

             the night in its hammock swinging the grouse to sleep.

To know buckthorn is to know the belly of a bear,
        the black flesh made new, the black path
to the ice trees where cloud is breath ... is salt ... is swan.

           (And the quiet plum won't say a word.)

The dwarf pine blossoms only after fire.
        This is not a fruit but a way of disappearing,
a flame caught red-handed in the infinite brown grass

            where the poison ivy lives, itself a fruit for starling

and wren, and for the skin of mouths our bodies
        speak of: blister, ooze, and forgivable sin.

iii. String Figures and How to Make Them

Bend the rind of an orange, the Inuit say,
        and you will see its true breath, darting
into the cold world.

They call the orange *eye of God*, and believe
        that it lives with the eels among the bloody waters.
Not anymore, of course. It is only an orange now.

Eventually, truth gives up its names and settles

down for the evening with a smoke and a beer.
I've learned this much.

In November you begin to know how long
        the winter will be, and that the evening
is rather a lonesome place.

        (I laugh at it in order not to die from it.)

The first snow turns blue and sighs
        against the birches, the black willows,
as it should. There is nothing else to see, and we move on.

The truth comes to me only when I am alone,
        but even then, it's hard to tell what is truth
and what is the ashen light through storm clouds.

I never learned much about the Inuit. Sealskin,
        whalebone, the myth of the one hundred names
for snow. It all seemed unreal, too close

        to a pure solitude I would never feel in my life.

But imagine their first taste of that other world,
        years ago after the American freighter sank,
a lifeboat filled with oranges, the only survivors.

Imagine what one orange could do to such a solitude,
        that calm, silent truth of froth and rime,
then imagine a boat full of oranges, a radiance

unlike anything they had ever seen upon the sea,
                a gift from the eyes of God,

and the children playing string figures on the shore,

calling sinew into names:
Cat's Cradle. Moving Spear. Lightning. Stars.

iv. The Grand Banks of Newfoundland

Roethke once said, *The spirit says: You are nothing.*
        And I'm not sure who to believe ...
Roethke or the spirit?

North of everywhere, Newfoundland waits
        for the blackberries to thaw, to ensanguine
grass and niche. It knows nothing of the spirit,

        and remains nothing.

Fossiled fish gather in the sod, rummage through
        trunks and ice. It is all right with me to know
that my life is only one life ... it will not multiply.
                It will not last.

I can say this honestly for the first time,
        not as confession but as solace.
Today the creek that runs through this island

was brimmed with yellow leaves, and I want to say
        that I felt some sort of shift in the light
drifting to the marsh, a loosening of
                the mind that comes with winter ...

as if this place could rise beyond the abandoned sea
        and take what is hers.

Dear Newfoundland,
        crate your doves and send them home.

The rats that throw themselves from your cliffs
        are the same pink things you once held
softly in your hand, before the sea
        carved the whale's hide.

From what twilight does this white air break,
        alone beside the gentle nets?

Here is where your first daughter drowned,
        torn by the moon's withered arms.
She took your wedding dress down the minnow-road,
        and sold it to the crabs, dirt-cheap.

There is nothing I can say to make you feel any better.
Forgive me.   The yellow leaves have met the sea.
        No one will be saved.

v. Favorite Songs of the 1890s

No one remembers them.
           Don't even try.

In the attic of the old Dover Books building,
        moths have chewed through the camphor,
the lavender veils,
        and are crowding the air with larva.

This is how it works:
        no moth wants a song,
so they eat what makes the sound,
        and there's nothing left.

Ta-Ra-Ra-Boom-De-Aye,
        Under the Bamboo Tree,
Bird in a Gilded Cage ...

... the kinds of songs that made Idaho
        join the Union and Wyoming weep
its way across the Tetons in freight cars
                full of buckshot and rabies.

They're long gone — lost to the moths'
        silken stomachs, to the sleet
swirling the rafters.

But what of *The Band Played On*
        or *After the Ball?*
Try *cadaver*, from the Latin *cadere*,
                which means *to fall*.

And this book? A medical student
        dissecting a dead decade under kerosene
lanterns, the light on the body humming
                a sick and golden tune.

No matter what, the night that lives inside the night
        goes deeper into the history of damage,
of erasure, of the one thousand
                tentative wings that swarm our eyes

and the moon's ungodly throat shines
        like neglect on the street,
a gentle, quiet poverty for the winter
                that bears our lives.

vi. The Fitzwilliam Virginal Book

Today, the sky is the color of a pigeon's throat,
not the roof of wild pear. And the light
a sluggish vellum that gauzes the mountain
and the fields below it ... the cow pond
cowless, weighted with leaves turning
the water slowly black, so when winter comes,
the ice knows where to go.
All that decrescendo, from sky to ice,
isn't going to get us anywhere.
There's no passion in it, no star
to navigate the pyre of wasp nests
in the orchard. It reminds me of my sister, years
ago, furious at the piano, her small hands cramping
the notes meant for a four hundred year-old
harpsichord. *Morley, Byrd, Bull, Gibbons.*
Names that would haunt her all summer
with intonation only ghosts compose.
Modern notation or not, it swarmed our house,
the 17th century deep in the dog's mouth,
the goldfish bowl, in the Red-headed
Woodpecker hammering on the shingles.
Even our father, who feared nothing
but sleep, escaped to the pine bower
to soak his ears in sap.
There are songs that have saved lives,
and songs that have ended them.
These were neither.
I'm not complaining.
I want, just this once,
for the air to clear and the night
come down to me like it used to,

there under the pines, as I watched
my father close his eyes against the evening,
the piano a distant wind over the marshes,
both of us straining to hear the blossoms
of my sister's arms wilt and crumble.

DOCUMENTING THE BIRDS

LETTER TO ALLISON WITH MUSICAL NOTATION OF HAWK

I'm going to pretend that you're dead. I'm going to use
that feeling to get somewhere else.
                    — Alice Aycock

Turn, trill, staccato, pause.

      Night can be herons, a barn or snow.
             A halo shifting the moon.

      Once, I found the wing of a hawk in a trough of light.

(There are traces left by wings
        and we carry them with us.)

Forget the angels: in the haymow of an abandoned barn,
      I saw the truest version of a soul,
           and held it to my face to see the ants
drift among the feathers.

      Night can be rivers, or grass.

If this were summer, the fireflies
      would lift the silos away
           from their white bodies and the owls.

But it is winter, the earth's shadow
      a slow flock across the moon.

And once, I saw the face of God on a sleeping girl,
      her hair the edge of the forest in dusk,

          and I could not turn away.

Allison, the oaks on our street
are rotting from too much rain.
                        Be careful of sudden winds.

I will not pretend that you're dead.

There is snow here, and a night so cold
                it hurts to breathe, it hurts to live.

DOCUMENTING THE BIRDS: OFFICE PARK

If this is what we become
        then let me turn into light now while the spaces
between the leaves have enough room to hold me.

        There are dead birds everywhere.
It's the windows of these buildings that get them,
        mirrored, mimicking versions of a better sky

full of the wind-strung trees of late summer,
        or the hibiscus red of blurred traffic lights.
A Black-chinned Hummingbird,

        its throat broken and pink, is the latest.
To hold its body, bare-handed, is to hold air,
        the green-clothed breath murmuring among the groves.

There have been Canada Geese, rising from the asphalt lake
        and splitting themselves open, leaving a thick *V* of spit on the glass.
Last week, it was the same Chimney Swift, twice,

        with a chattering flourish, its eyes full of the nothing
that comes with this place. The first time didn't do the job,
        the second took both wings off, as if to enter this new sky,

to be a flame in this dusk, requires an exchange of desire.
        For each wing of a swift a sycamore must fall, somewhere
under our breath and between the cities of our closing eyes.

        In his journals, Audubon talked of a hollow sycamore
full of swifts, hundreds of them. An ocean of wings.
        And how, after he put his ear to the bark, he watched a farmer

set the tree on fire to rid his land of the birds.
        The birds would not leave the tree so they became it,
blackened and soaring under the furrows.

The worst: a lost pet Canary in the parking lot,
its feet amputated by a weed-eater.
		The Canary couldn't understand why its feet

were no longer tucked below, and so it hovered
		above them until its wings gave out.
What I know about Canaries isn't much.

		I held one once for a quarter at a county fair,
and in its brightness it held me, a child dumb beneath a living flame,
		the husks of its clipped wings rustling in the shadows

 of the parachutes. And there's the story of my father's Matilda,
		who could write the letter *M*
on the butcher-block paper lining her cage

		with a tiny pencil in her beak.
The same lazy and shaken *M* a blind girl would carve
		into a picnic table to mimic the feel

of her classmates' words deep across the wood.
		There are many kinds of sickness, I know,
and the women's white dresses billow and cling to their legs

		as they stroll around this lake at lunch because
that is how things happen, the wind blows and fills us,
		but what if time is the illness?

What if the plentiful burst from being so many at once?
		Audubon said that the only real number is one,
the rest are mere repetition. I admit to believing him at times,

		the third-person fading into a sort of artificial twilight,
the air in flames all around us not really air anymore
		but a small bright space between the leaves.

The raspy screech of the Barn Owl is now the fax machine,
        the coffee maker's incessant drip is the nasal *peent*
of a Nighthawk, calling his lover home.

        Even the singular truth of a Red-headed Woodpecker's beak
against the sycamore became Audubon's knife
        at the black heart of the wood, because to matter,

here in this field of bricked glass, there must be
        evidence of a life, a narrowing, a slimming down,
tailored to fit the body of air a hand could hold.

        One mantle, one nape, one crown, one crest.
The Great Blue Heron wading in the lake doesn't count yet
        as it lifts one leg in front of the other,

over a plastic bag and onto the sidewalk where we sit
        and eat our perfect lunches, talking of the trees,
the glad and empty trees.

BURNING INSTEAD OF BEAUTY

In an autumn fog, it is easy to mistake a falling leaf for a sparrow,
          the simple brown of their backs: hollow-boned meadow.
A pale branch of seed in its beak, a string of feed corn.

Or, a stem so thin the air becomes the stem, and a beak
          would only mean that something is warm behind it,
and what good is that in autumn when the leaves
          become the little sisters of sparrows?

But think of the fog, how it must feel when it peels back
          from the valley only to find a leaf that is a sparrow,
a sparrow that is a leaf. Consider that, when the fog
          edges toward the sea, the sea is no longer itself.

It remains the valley, a part of the land.
          It becomes a field of white blossoms blown
from the tree of wind, from the trawler's nets,
          and as we walk the boiled lip of the beach
the fog thickens and we become less and less ourselves
          and for a moment we are lost among the waves,
among the leaves, and we've really gone nowhere
          but it feels like something has happened, that we've gone beyond
everything, that our bodies, fragile and alone,
          are finally where they need to be.

It's a false voyage, of course, because when the body
          is no longer ours, we take from it.

How dull and purple it is, raked clean, sponged and sewn.
          Sad even, in its own way, when it finally becomes just a body,
and we return to what reminds us of it.

Heart: oxen knee-deep in a canal.
　　　Tissue: blanket of silt, blanket of snow.
Lung: tracks of an otter through an oyster bed.
　　　Brain: monsoon ... cello strings ... the beginnings of songs.

None of this really brings us back to what we once knew,
　　　but we try, and in trying, there is decay.
When the body becomes a stem, a leafy dome of air,
　　　we crowd around our nothingness and stutter,
pretending we see the bird cages of our chests rise and fall,
　　　pretending that it is easy to go on without having
what we have always had. Easy because ...

Easy because decay slowly begins with our body's beginning.

It is slow enough for my brother's body to be facedown
　　　in the pond, to remember the turtles napping on his back
as if he were a tiny whitened log bleached by the sun,
　　　the mosquitoes gathering up his fingers.

Slow enough to be 17 again, making love
　　　on the beach with a girl who would forget me
by autumn, a girl who could kiss the kiss of a paper bird,
　　　and the trawlers offshore flashing their spotlights
into the fog beyond the one-mile marker, the slight gleam
　　　of mackerel in their nets enough to make us grab the blanket
to cover up our bodies bright against the rising tide:
　　　the crumbled outline of a refugee's boat:
all four of our lungs breathing in as much as we can.

To remember which of my father's lungs was given
　　　to the man in Sweden who has almost lost his body,
the retinas sent by helicopter to Ohio for the child
　　　who will grow with pieces of my father in her.

Before we leave the body, the fog will cover us.

       We will bathe in its memory, facedown in the memory
of our beginning, our end, and every child in Ohio I meet

       from now on will be named *Father*
and I will see myself in them and I will love them,

       their dirty faces, their thin bodies warm and feathered,
fluttering in the breeze above the world while my father,

       empty, unknowing, keeps on giving himself away.

THE STIGMATA RATHER THAN A PUNCH ON THE NOSE

If you'd asked my father when he was nine
why he beat up a kid for calling him Little Bo Peep

he would have beat you up too. Not because
you would ask in that superior way you always do

but because he couldn't understand the difference
between hate and pain and for that he'd sock you one.

It had nothing to do with being a bonnet-headed
shepherdess forever afraid of wolves or communists

hiding in the chicken-coop, forever coming home
empty-handed. It was the destruction

of the one word he knew better
than any other that got to him.

Imagine: 1952, summer, an over-ripe pear
in each pocket, furiously defending his name

and his nose and no sheep in sight
down the sweet-leaf rows, no relief

for the wretched in Maysville, N.C.
He tried to picture himself leaving town

on the sorrel's dewed back, early morning,
the long-throated birds asleep in the sourgrass

and the sorrel wading into the horizon,
but all he could think of was a wonderful scene

in a movie and as always would become a spectator
of his own life. You would have thought

that the other boys (Marion and Steamboat and the rest),
shirt-tails open in the wind, would let up,

forget about it. They kept coming,
waiting for him on the back road beneath the willows.

Their fascination with seeing blood pour from a nose,
even their own, became not just blood

but the reconstruction of it.
Not love, but the forgetting:

a yellowed calm breaking over the leaves
and their faces as dusk did then.

This was not dusk or locust though.
It was the yellow that memory

brings to a place, carrying a kerosene lantern
lit for a boy stuck on the roof

of a grain silo, too afraid to climb down in the dark.
The yellow my father saw in his fists

as he would light up one boy after another
like a cupped match, making whoever it was pay

for the blood of his good name.
Little Bo Peep. Poteat.

It was a simple mistake to make,
but what does reason have to do with instinct,

with a stain on a boy's palm, the sow in her trough
bleeding out of her eyes for want of darkness

or rather a light luminous enough to see
the pear trees at the rim of the meadow

one last time? The sick sow he fed mornings,
combing the lice from her brow,

speaking his own name as a question to her. *Poteat?*
Our ruins follow us, that much he told me,

later, after our good-byes and our kind sirs
quickened in the clay, red at the heart of it,

the deepest well of it, the sow that rubbed
her ears raw on a fence post, long gone by then.

Calm yourself. Give in.
And that is where you find him, in the fields,

a muslin of rain delivering the ancient scent
of tobacco. Where else would he be?

Born in a field at the edge of a ditch, he would tell her.
This is a story without surprises.

The formality of a swallow's nest falling
from the ruined rafters of a silo didn't confuse

or sadden him, he just didn't want it anymore:
the dying becoming dead, and the dear old summer

washed up on the river's bank,
dear sweet summer.

The stupid pig lying there. *Fuck you. Fuck you.*
You don't know him at all.

LAMENT FOR A RUIN (CURLES NECK DAIRY FARM)

Give winter nothing.
      It doesn't care what we do.

It desires only a pure, silent field,
      between husk and hoof print,
the river and the hills.

One or the other, origin or sediment,
           it doesn't matter.

I say this now, watching the river ice
      ride toward the eastern towns
that will drown themselves by century's end,

        because even winter cannot stop me
from loving this place.

—

I have never loved a ruin.

My father was close, though his only ruin
      was his left leg, torn by a land mine
as he bent down to pull a leech from his ankle,
        a souvenir from scenic Vietnam.

He didn't blame the leech.

He just picked shrapnel from his skin
      for twenty years, and never admitted
how the pain carried him to the dark water
        of a winter he never knew he wanted.

What lives the dead keep within them,
      what astonishment of the body.

Or maybe not astonishment, not even close.

He would have called it an instructive hell,
          a solitude. And that's what winter wants.

To reclaim the solitude it eases over
          the open land, each ditch a jewel of insignificance,
each leaf on its way to the river of harm.

—

Winter is a vast space of distances,

and within that space, there is an abandoned farm,
          held together with the mud houses of wasps,
with the spit and twigs of swallows.

A fox den in the barn floor, the mother
                    waiting for the rabbit hour.

—

It has been said that a landscape shuns its trees
          in winter, looking straight through the branches
to the hills ahead, and the road between.

I'm not sure who said it, but it seems reasonable,
          although the landscape owns nothing — because,
of course, nothing remains. The bulldozers

                    that will carry away the silos are idling now
in the ditches, in the dead reeds — the limestone
          beneath these fields aches to know the wind again.

And here I am, one more day in my life
          almost gone, back in these fields

too proud to name themselves
                    and the frost that covers them.

A witness to the end of ... something.
          A century of milk and work and life
that had nothing to do with me.

———

Hurry, fox, tell me how to bleed the dusk,
          to peel away this sky and throw it back
to the land whole. I have seen your red face in the trees,
             the six mice of dawn
         sleeping in your mouth.

There is nothing that you can say to hurt me.

———

The swallows welcome each other in the eaves like snow.
This should not be mistaken for a kind of beauty,
        for it is not, and refuses it, like snow.

Pull from the hives a sweeter air to feed this land a sky,
         they say, or at least that's what they should say.

Dumb birds, get out while you can.
                Tonight, there will be nothing left.

———

I should have begun with one thing,
         one true object that will remain true,
one that cannot waver, cannot fail.

A severed wing of a hawk in a trough of light.

A swallow's nest, hanging from the tip of a rope
                              in an empty silo.

A hollowed hormone syringe
        among the blackberry vines,
among the long rows
            where the standing cows slept.

                    ———

It's the hawk wing I keep coming back to,

and the sunlight that held it. Probably a Red-tailed,
        from the order *Falconiformes*, genus *Buteo*.

            Never mind the Latin ... that's my father talking.

This is the kind of thing that can't be named,
        so I will sit here and listen, and think of St. Brigid,
patron saint of dairy farms, who drowned herself

            in a vat of rotted milk so she could shut out
the voices calling her to the wasp-black persimmons.

She wallowed with the cows, early morning, the dogs
        not yet awake, the workers still in their straw beds,
cramped fingers working the udderless air.

If there is a god, show yourself.

The calves have opened the gate,
and there is nothing between them
and the sea.

—

The sky does not mind the three silos, the five barns.
Neither does the sycamore that weaves shirts
for the air, its white bark the kind of death
that winter can appreciate.

For ten years, my father has been a true ruin,
one that no longer exists.

Ground to ashes and given to the sea
as sort of a gift — to him, rather, and not the sea.
The sea doesn't need us. Winter, either.

All true ruins depend upon disappearance,
the gradual slipping away into tissue and memory,
and since memory ruptures, and tissue rots,
there is a guarantee.

The sycamore knows this,
and gives the frail weeds under its boughs
the chance to last a few more nights.

—

This is going nowhere. What's the use?
One more father thrown to the fishes.

I promised myself to leave him alone. No more,
and here he is again,
at the wheel of a bulldozer after the first snow,
orange overalls and a shrug. *So what?*

When I try to imagine another life for him, I can't.

This is a weakness, I know.
        To watch him like this,
unaware, is also a weakness.

But he's here whether I like it or not
        with his heavy equipment license,
passing around a thermos of coffee and scotch,
                his breath visible once again, his limp
not so bad thanks to a couple of Darvon, a plastic brace.

I've always thought we should put our ghosts to work.
        All those callused, transparent hands eager
for one simple act to remain part of the living.

So let the silos fall, if this is what it takes.

Let the swallows with spoons in their beaks
dig through the barns for their impossible eggs,

the wasp larva writhe under the rusted pitchforks,
                the wingless hawk sleep soundly

in the wind of its own undoing,

and let the fox and her two kits trot away,
        refusing to look back, refusing to believe

that it all meant something more than what it was.

And what of the Snowy Owl roosting
        in the tin roof of the silo,
the one that stared down as I tested

my own pale voice against the inner walls,

the one that lined the dirt floor with mice skulls
        and rabbit's pelt as if to say,
Welcome, you're dead now.

It could have been the entrance to the city
        of the dead, there in the silo, the curved white
walls not concrete but blocks of human ash.

Yes, it was the owl's eyes,
        bruised and round and full of a beauty
this world needs, and doesn't get.

I will not say they were the eyes of my father,
                although I would like to.

Anyone would, but not now, not here.
                This is not for him. I promise.

This is for the farm, my one great ruin,
        my patron saint of limestone and blight,

my angel of extinction, my winter's shattered leg,
                my sycamore shirt, my river of husks,

my owl heart, my cow's ear, my one last look,

and dear god I picked up that hawk's wing,
        high in the haymow, and I swear

it was the truest version of light I had ever seen,

and held it to my face to see the ants
                drift among the feathers,

and it would not fly away,

        it would not leave me in the cold winds,

it would not forget and carry my one life

        all night through the quiltless and unending snow.

THE BLACK SCAFFOLDS OF WING
COME APART WITH THE DAYS

SELF-PORTRAIT AS THE AUTUMN I HAVE LOST

Believe me, if I knew a better way to put this
   I would, but this is the best I can do:
when I was ten, I derailed a train.

   There. I said it. It wasn't much to think about.
How can you honestly think about something like that?

   It just happens. You pick the stones up, or you push them
onto the tracks. Or you can use the rotted ties

   lying beside the track, the ones the track-layers
would take shits on. Either way, it'll work.

   Either way, your hands will get dirty, but what I think of
the most is the freight car full of pigs,

   their perfect white feet rising in the dusk.

JUST FOR YOU

I'm beginning to understand the moon,
      the way the years disembody themselves
from it. Not ghost, not heart, not mulse or acacia,
        but a peach-borer moth, wings of slate-colored

gauze, its flight a messy thing, incinerator ash
      over a pond well-tuned with the music of frogs
and everywhere great patches of irised air
      like horse-mint in the fields

or the rose-bloom of the wild bean.
      The moon's light is not its own.
The moth knows this and maybe that is what
      the perpetual shimmer of the peach trees

have been trying to say all June. Not, *All is peace*
      but, *Poor moon this will never be yours.*
To translate light into form isn't quite enough, really.
      The world hurts as it is, lit, swelled.

To untie a dead raven strung up with copper wire in an orchard
      isn't enough, either. Look how the black scaffolds of wing
come apart with the days. Twenty years from now I might only remember
      this bird among the dark fruit, the bare unending solitude

of its wing and there's nothing that can be done about it. Light loosens,
      ripens through branches, a bloom. The moth asks to be born
from a peach, from telephone poles graphing the blunt
      edges of streets. In exchange, it gives up its gauze

to the sky, kind moth, and with gray winds evening comes.
      The moon has wings, too, don't forget,
or hands, the perfect hands of air, work-gloves burning in a pile
      of leaves. *I am only I.*

After a dream of dancing trees, Whitman awoke
    and wrote down what he could remember
of the curious promenade, *With a whisper from one*
     bending down as he pass'd me

"We do all this on the present occasion exceptionally,
    just for you."

As does the moon in its best season of devotion,
    not mend, not change,
not the moth's white cloak of light,
     not calm, not raven's breath,

but Calf. Blind.
    Flower. Seed
Eyed. Faced.
     Shine. Struck.

SONATA FOR AN OPEN WINDOW

i.

Look. This photograph ...
It always begins with a photograph, doesn't it?
Monsieur Daguerre hiding in the chinaberry trees
while the crowd of mothers with their dying babies
wept on his front lawn for him and his camera,
his silvered trays of bromine and iodine that could hold children
in their fever, in their vomit-stained smocks,
and never let them go. And the whole time Daguerre,
among the trees, was thinking of Cuba, the early morning light
against the sides of white houses, the glare of the ocean
at noon, the flicker of a ship's polished railing
through the leaves of a palm.

So look at this, then. For his sake.
It is me: the ghost of me: nine months before I am me.
It is the summer of 1962, and my mother is leaning out of a window,
her hair pulled back, reaching for the branch of a cherry tree
as you would tack a sail to catch a west wind.
The wavering sheet of blossoms, the push of twilight billowing around her.
A simple photograph. Nothing fancy.

And what it comes down to is this: it is Albany, New York.
She has just graduated from high school.
The nuns have told her that all things are fire. The trees
through the window are merely flame, and to fall from the window
would mean giving up what has not happened yet
to the lawn graying in the sun just out of the photograph,
just as much there as the blossom falling from her hand.

—

It is 1962. That much is certain, and Cuba is in love.
With itself. With Manzanillo, Santa Clara,
Cienfuegos, their palms, their plates of paella
cold and uneaten. With the gas lanterns that line the villages
near the bay. With all the old thieves that play dice outside
the brothels in Havana and knife each other in the alleys.
With two young thieves offshore stealing crabs
from wooden traps. Their boat made from banana crates,
its rigging, their daughter's dresses. They are drunk on coconut wine,
and still, Cuba loves them.
And it is in love with the cigar makers
asleep in their shoes on the roof of the Hotel Matanzas,
the roll of their fingers caught up in the moment, the making.
The wild pigs in the forests, the pigs in the butcher's window.
The song of the child counting out grains of rice into clay jars.
All of it.

But the road to Carderras is caving in, and soon, there will be nothing left.
There are dogs gathering in the square. There are soldiers on the roofs
picking out the houses they will live in and the women that will love them.
The trees through the window have always been flame, and soon
Cuba will no longer be in love.

The face of my mother in a window, gasoline
in a bottle. How could she have known that fire can last
only so long? That before the photograph was taken,
before she reached for the blossoms, before she smiled
at the thought of falling into the branches and resting there,
her face became mine for a moment.

What did she know of Cuba then? That it is only ash
and rum, a kettle burning (and love, if it can be called that,
is a leaf pressed in a book).
Maybe pineapples, or the dark men, their white shirts on clotheslines

hanging over the streets. Maybe that is not the right question.
What did Cuba know of her? That it hated her. Well, yes.
That America is nothing more than a barn with an old blind mule
tied to a post, biting at any close and sudden movement, mostly biting itself.
Yes, that too.

ii.

And here I am, thirty years later, in that Cuba she never knew.
It is hotter than she would have thought, and there's a sound
that I can't quite place coming in from the sea, like the bells
of a cathedral, a morning fog slowly fading.
Would it help if I told you Daguerre took the photos of the babies
in their mother's thin, white arms and kept them
for himself: a wall of dying babies in his studio
to remind him of what he had done, of what he had become?
That he had never even heard of Cuba?

I would be lying if I did.

To come here was a mistake. I know it, now.
Listening to the couple from Ohio
in the bungalow next door make love last night,
the woman high-pitched, a chickadee, and the man
never saying anything at all, I felt the glorious pain
of being alone. You know that pain? You, asleep beside me,
as close as you could get, and yet I was alone.
I could feel your breath on my arm.
I didn't want to be here, and of all the things
I could have thought, I thought of that photograph
of my mother, the one with her in the window
of her parents house on Third Street, of how she looked
almost like me, of how, if it was me instead of her,
I would never leave that window or those white blossoms.
I would have become one of the blossoms, faded into winter,

and pressed myself into a book.
What a stupid thing to think, but I did, and I got up and walked
to the window to look out onto the sea and the night beyond it.
I wanted to say something about the sky, how wide and swirling
and completely beyond us it was, but you were asleep,
and I could not stop any of it, so I said it anyway.

The river birches burned that year.
The fire jumped the river and took down both sides,
a mile each way. The wooden shells of the warehouses,
the furnace factory, the docks and the *That's All Benny*
(the only patrol cruiser that made it back from the war without a dent)
all burned with the birches. Then it rained.

The Hudson rose and would not stop and the fire, the Great Hudson Fire,
was out and my mother could speak again, lying on her bed,
reading the cracks in the ceiling: a capsized boat, two drunken men
leaning on each other wrapped in the dress of a sail,
their faces identical, their faces hers.
Disasters made her speechless, and sad, and even beautiful,
I have been told. The brilliance of her hair against the summer sky through
a bedroom window ... the river rose and Albany rose and she wondered
when it would stop, wondered when, if the end came, the city would
give up its flicker and groan to the river and become a mountain.

Can it be that she did not understand any of this?
That a disaster on top of a disaster becomes absurd,
and the only thing to do was laugh, and imagine yourself
far away, maybe on a beach, somewhere where there might be trees
with blossoms all year around.
That my birth, when it came months later, was beyond the burning
of logs, the coals washed out and solid on the banks of the Hudson,
my father wrapping her in a blanket to keep the mosquitoes off,
and me suddenly there, a thin candle's flame in her womb.

If there was a choice, I might have chosen to remain there
on that beach between the campfire and the slim gusts of wind
that took me from absence to combustion,
between the Cuba that is far away and loved,
and the dark cloud of sea.

But I am here now, with you, the product of a summer night
and a trough beside the remnants of bonfires, dug in, kicked over.

Maybe it is better to not be born just yet.
Maybe if she steps back from the window,
she will see that women are shaped like leaves
and men fall. A month before the photograph,
she will meet my father for the first time
under the awning of a movie theater,
and realize that need must be spoken:
a crawfish burrowing into the mud.

In Cuba, they do not bury the dead.
They keep them in rooms, and talk
about them, as if they are not there.
Remember the trail to the bay?
Inside those tiny huts of tin cans?
All dead. Those creeks leaf-choked?
Dead. Sometimes it is that simple.
A word. A whisper. You can only have so much.

The clay jar of rice you hid on the top shelf
was found and searched this morning.
The soldiers ... they have nothing else to do.
It is almost a game to them. They miss loneliness
so they take it from us. They want to know where everything is
at all times, and that thirst keeps them going.

There is, of course, no need for dreams here.
They come and go, without cause or want, and become others
the next door down, the same one over and over.
The palm-leafed roofs let out the cooking smoke,
the cooking fires bronzed with salted plats of wood,
and the children play with their wooden figures of the Apostles
found on the beach when the American ship sank.
Enrique the grocer wants to know if you still need
the white pineapples you asked him to save for you.
Tell him, when you come back from the village,
that pineapples are nothing, that his country makes me sick,
that tomorrow the tide is coming in higher than ever before.

iii.

Albany, 6 p.m., and violence is everywhere. My mother, scratched
by her cat that can almost speak her name. *Dianne, Dianne.*
Her father, lump-headed from a fallen wash-tub, a creaking shelf.
Her brother, the ice cream truck's door, a broken nose.

The shore of the river collects what it can for the winter,
for the long path to the ocean. There is a candle in the window
of the bowling alley, lit for the birches on the riverbank,
for the president, for the ships waiting offshore from Havana.

My mother walks by the river, and tries to skip stones
across its weightless back.
They sink, and nothing changes.
She lights a cigarette, the smoke-drifts of her mouth a ripple.
Two field sparrows above her, on the branch
of a blackened cherry tree, watch her trace the cigarette
in the air, writing her name, her questionable conversations,
into a burning arc of light.

They see something in the river, a clump floating near the opposite shore,
and they sing to it. Reflection of warehouses, street lamps:
her own blurred body an open window: she speaks to it.

But doesn't know what to do, or what to make of it.
A dead body? Walk away? Dip her feet?

So she stands and lets it rise around her, the stumps of barrels
and sewer pipes drifting in their own rust. It is this simple.
The rising, the falling. What could anyone do but stand and let it happen?

It is still 1962. There is no changing that. She is seventeen.
Change becomes her. She will attend nursing school this winter
and see for the second time a dead body, and she'll tug at the eyelashes
to close the eyes. She will ask the doctors whether or not hair keeps
growing after we die, but not what she wants to ask, which is whether
a cigarette's flame can bring back the color of the Hudson on fire,
or what she wants to know, which is whether the child inside her can feel
the warm swirl of night growing around it. So many questions,
and Guantanamo is just washing out its nightshirts,
the dark skins of the women's backs on fire.

—

You, under the bed, picking each grain of rice
back into its jar, look. The sun is setting.
I won't talk about the photograph anymore.
It was silly of me.

Watch the soldiers in the street, smoking their cigars.
Or don't. I'm not making you.

Of course. I understand. The light is going.
You need it. There is only a certain amount of time
left for this, for us. You never met my mother,
who asked a surgeon to leave behind a photograph

of the Hudson in a tiny plastic capsule after
he sewed her up, so she couldn't forget.
If she were here, she would like you, that you smoke,
that your face is not as white as it seems. Go for a walk,
she would tell you. It puts color into your cheeks.

But what good is any of this? I want to know.
This morning, there was a wasp flitting from wall to wall
to the window's white framing of sky, and I wanted
to let it out, into the trees and into the sails on the bay
in the distance. Then, for some reason, I began to like the idea
of it bouncing from the walls, confused with the whiteness
or just tired of looking for the window, as if bouncing
could help it find a way out, as if it could slip itself
between the white and the window and find the trees
shining in the bright day, fall into them, and wait
for the sad motion of rain to come and wash it away.

What good is that wasp when it is no longer 1962?
It is thirty years later, a dead husk of wings on the sill.
Must I tell you this? It has always been thirty years later.
Always Cuba and Albany.

Even now, when I look at you, it is thirty years,
and what the nuns told my mother is a cup of leaves.
Thirty years is thirty years, and what have I become,
holding this dead wasp up to the light?

I am going to say what the sea would say to me, which is
nothing can become more than it is.
I am going to say what my mother would say to me,
but I have forgotten her voice, hovering above
the blossoming trees, the drowning city. It is hard to admit, this forgetting.
The bananas ripening on the table, pin-drops of rice into a jar.

Let us part here.
Maybe it is better to spend the night alone.
The walk back is too long. There are shapes of water
on the walls of the white buildings.
Your sandals are falling apart. You won't make it.
Sit here and watch the ships, the hills above the village,
the wind (or is it the soldiers?) pushing open each red door
of the bungalows, and the scent of lemon trees curling inland.
It is something to remember.

Shaped from the grayed edge of flame, this becomes
what it is supposed to become. Memory. A photograph.
A souvenir. A measurement of the unsaid,
lingering and wind-filled. Over the sea: the root of smoke:
within the star: the trembling world.

Louis Daguerre was nothing but iodine on a sheet
of copper warming in the sun, tugging at his own eyelashes
under a portrait of his mother on the banks of the Seine,
parasol sagging from a morning rain,
and I am not where I need to be.

Maybe it is better for you here, in this Cuba of your eyes,
where every woman leaning out of a window
to empty her washbowl has my mother's face,
where all the dresses are white and rented
and all the white pineapples in the market
are free if you know what to say,
if you can speak the tongue of sickles, of sugarcane.
Wait. Let me tell you something before you go, a story.
There was a river, once.
A boy holding his mother's dead hand.
There were men's faces in the trees.

THE NOSTALGIA OF THE FINITE

Remember those women in the movies
       who wept into the hair of their dead men?
The crumbled red walls of their voices,
         shored on a riverbank? I was young then,

and to remember the glow of willows
       above the women, the snails under their feet,
the mule hobbled and fly-bitten,
        is to remember what slips away.

Well, at least I'll try to remember.
        It's important not to neglect such things.
The weeping ... yes, that's important,
        but what comes after the weeping

and the birch-bark love letters
       is the white screen of fog,
the mule asleep in the rain.
        No, I haven't forgotten.

Sometimes the men would keep
       their eyes open so the women could see
that it wasn't that hard to drown,
        to show them that to have seen the bottom

of a river is to have seen the end,
       what the living call *light* or *silence*
or *the village with its darkened blue roofs.*
        Sometimes the women would look

at the men, bundles of frozen reeds,
       and remember what it was like to walk together
through the cut fields of wheat beyond
        the village, to drink from the same jar,

to sleep and know that under the morning's eaves,
           all women are one woman: all men, one man.
The dark theater, an usher waking you.
                  The end so plainly there, it hurts just to see it.

NOTES

NOCTURNE: FOR THE RIVER

"Participate joyfully in the sorrows of the world," is borrowed from Joseph Campbell, who borrowed it from Buddha. The brief account of Whitman's post-war visit to Richmond is loosely based on his collection of journals, *Specimen Days*. Special thanks to *Nebraska Review* for awarding this their annual Editor's Prize, and for nominating it for a Pushcart Prize.

NOCTURNE: FOR THE NIGHT WORKERS OF THE SOUTH

Christ did not say, "You are what you eat," although he could have, I guess. Influenced by Richard Avedon's early photographs of asylum patients. The bird legends are loosely based on *The Bird Artist*, by Howard Norman. The last italicized lines are from Whitman's *Specimen Days*.

DAMNATIO MEMORIAE

The lines, "Let's be sentimental for once, let's return to the authentic," are from Bruno Shultz's *Sanatorium under the Sign of the Hourglass*.

Special thanks to Adam Chiles and Susan Megson.

HITCHHIKING IN THE DYING SOUTH

The opening two stanzas owe gratitude to Gaston Bachelard's *The Poetics of Space* and the rest to Hampstead, N.C.

Special thanks to everyone at *Blackbird* for taking this and six others.

MEDITATIONS IN THE MARGINS
OF THE BOOK OF IRISH CURSES

Curses taken from *The Book of Irish Curses*, edited by Patrick C. Power.
IV. is the title of a sculpture by Alice Aycock. The line "... hail to whatever you found in the sunlight that surrounds us ..." was kindly stolen from Rilo Kiley's second record on the Saddle Creek label. This one is for Allison, as per usual.
VI. is for the adult home guys on Grace.
VII. is indebted to John Cheever's journals, and to eBay's medical antiques section.
VIII. sounds like a bad version of a Police song, and I apologize.
IX. is for Oregon Hill.

Special thanks to Nicole Cooley, for awarding sections of this the *River City* poetry prize, and to American Poetry Archives/San Francisco State University's Poetry Center for awarding other sections the Rella Lossy Prize.

FAHRENHEIT MEDITATION
    For Adam and Emily Chiles.

    The Alexander the Great quote "Sir Barons . . ." comes from Celeste Olalquiaga's
    book, *The Artificial Kingdom*.

GRASS MEDITATION
    Owes gratitude to Theodore Roethke, and Marilynne Robinson's *Housekeeping,* of
    which the first two lines of section 1 are from.

    For my grandmother Mary Shearer.

MEDITATION FOR THE DEAD SWISS
    Titled after the artist Christian Boltanski's installation, *The Dead Swiss.*

SELF-PORTRAIT AS THE AUTUMN OF THE RED HAT
    Titled after Romare Bearden's collage *Autumn of the Red Hat* in the collection of
    the Virginia Museum of Fine Arts.

    Special thanks to Richard Howard for awarding this the *Columbia* Poetry Prize,
    and to former editor of *Columbia*, Rangi McNeil.

PEOPLE WHO'D KILL ME
    Influenced by Victor Erice's 1973 film, *El Espíritu de la colmena (Spirit of the
    Beehive),* and my uncle Gordon Lovejoy, keeper of bees.

    Special thanks to Nicole Cooley for choosing this poem for the *Lullwater Review*
    Poetry Prize.

THE ANGELS CONTINUE TURNING THE WHEELS
OF THE UNIVERSE DESPITE THEIR UGLY SOULS
    Titled after an Alice Aycock sculpture.

    Greatly indebted to Robert Hobbs' writings on Aycock, to my chiropractor
    Clinton Kinnear, and to the beautifully haunted Malvern Hill. Special thanks to
    the folks at *Gulf Coast*.

    For Robert Hobbs and Jean Crutchfield.

OUR MEMORY, THE SHINING LEAVES
(WATERFORD FAIR CIVIL WAR REENACTMENT)
>Indebted to *Gardner's Photographic Sketch Book of the Civil War*, and to the town of Waterford, Va.

>For Lisa Kiernan, wherever she may be.

FROM THE 1941 CATALOGUE OF DOVER BOOKS
>All titles conveniently taken from the actual 1941 Catalogue of Dover Books. Thanks to Dover Books and to the lovely people at *Crazyhorse*.

>III. is for Anne Scallon.
>VI. is for my sister Kira Poteat.

DOCUMENTING THE BIRDS: OFFICE PARK
>Audubon did not actually say, "the only real number is one." That was Nabokov. Special thanks to David Lee for awarding this a *Bellingham Review* poetry prize.

LAMENT FOR A RUIN (CURLES NECK DAIRY FARM)
>The opening line, "Give winter nothing," is from James Wright's journals.

SELF-PORTRAIT AS THE AUTUMN I HAVE LOST
>The title taken from Fernando Pessoa's journals. Special thanks to Richard Howard for also awarding this one the *Columbia* Poetry Prize.

>For Jason Bishop.

JUST FOR YOU
>Whitman's dream of dancing trees is taken from his *Specimen Days*.

SONATA FOR AN OPEN WINDOW
>Greatly indebted to the Soviet/Cuban film, *I am Cuba* (*Soy Cuba/Ya Kuba*). Special thanks to Stephen Dobyns for awarding this the *Marlboro Review* Poetry Prize, and to editor Ellen Dudley.

THE NOSTALGIA OF THE FINITE
>The first two lines, "Remember those women in the movies who wept into the hair of their dead men," are from Federico Fellini's 1973 film, *Amarcord*.

>For my teacher Larry Levis.

INDEX OF BIRDS

ABOUT THE AUTHOR

Joshua Poteat has won awards from *American Literary Review, River City, Nebraska Review, Marlboro Review, Columbia, Bellingham Review, Yemassee, Lullwater Review,* Vermont Studio Center, Catskill Writing Workshop, American Poetry Archives/San Francisco State University, and Universities West Press. He won the 2004 National Chapbook Fellowship from the Poetry Society of America. In 2001, he was the Summer Writer-in-Residence at the University of Arizona's Poetry Center and, in 2002, was awarded an Individual Artist's Grant from the Virginia Commission for the Arts.

Blackbird: an online journal of literature and the arts featured him in their Spring 2003 issue. His poems have appeared in *Crazyhorse, Gulf Coast, The Greensboro Review, Lit,* and many others.

His work is part of a two-year international traveling exhibition, *Pivot Points,* featuring three generations of painters and poets, including Larry Levis, Dave Smith, and Gregory Donovan.

He grew up in the woods and marshes of Hampstead, North Carolina, and now lives in Richmond, Virginia, where he edits assorted texts, including art criticism and junk mail for credit card companies.

THE ANHINGA PRIZE
FOR POETRY SERIES